Poetry Songs

Cynthia Rose

To life

And

Love

Brave is the woman who

wanders but is not lost.

The crash of breaking worlds

will not trouble the heart that is

truly at peace.

Happiness is like

drinking wine sweetened with

Sunbeans.

There are times when I don't
want reality to catch my
daydreams.

Now that I'm older, the days

float by. Like bubbles they

glisten in the sunlight

and pop silently in midair.

Time is a teaser

dancing in a red dress

trimmed in gold.

Though I tread on stony ground

and stumble,

I won't stop; for I have

promises to keep.

*True friends can walk
in the garden of their minds and
pick bouquets of understanding.*

Within every person

is a kingdom;

for most, undiscovered and

uncharted.

I am haunted by human beings;

the greatness of their violence;

their vast and timid goodness

cowering in the shadows;

tiptoeing out

when it is safe.

In the eternal darkness

the dawn breaks.

Be patient.

They rose to success;

mocking the ones left behind.

The crash came,

and no one showed up

to break the fall.

When I swim in troubled

waters, the currents wrestle

me down

and teach me strength.

Your love

was fleeting as the snowflake

at first sun;

too beautiful to last.

God and Demon is Man;

spinning Heaven and Hell

on this blue ball in space.

Some things

I can't pray away.

So I'll ride the pain easy

until I reach the shore.

Thank you Mother Time

for not coming all at once;

for slow years of aging

that help me bare the wisdom

of seeing life clearly;

for not being too unkind

as I give up my illusions.

I asked for freedom

and it climbed on my back,

weighing me down

with responsibility.

Music

is the eternal quests

and timeless longings

of the heart.

When my time

has come and gone,

let me fly away easy.

The baby's newborn cry

carries the tides of every shore;

and the beat of

ancestral drums.

A breaking heart

makes no sound.

The Sunrise says,

"The best is yet to come."

The warrior became

introspective

and his heart softened

toward his enemy.

I want my life to be short

enough so I won't grow weary;

and long enough that I learn

what it is meant to teach me.

"Why do you stare at me?" asked the blade of grass. "I'm pondering my ignorance," said the wise man.

The eyes are cloudy.

The footsteps are slow;

The soul is stirring;

preparing to return home.

The noise turns to music

when we make peace with

ourselves.

The rich man with earned

ulcers looked with envy at the

pauper sitting on the ground

eating a bowl of beans.

Silence sits with me

and whispers anwers.

I see my face in foreign lands.

Wherever I go I am everyone.

In the fire of the dragon;

In the dark dungeon

dampened with despair;

In the belly of the beast

I've known mercy.

Without a song

the flight of the eagle could not

be. No blossoming of the rose;

No coming forth

of generations unborn;

without a song

The child comes to earth

carrying the work

she is meant to do;

fully equipped for complete

expression.

Without the thorn

the rose could not be

Here comes that rainy day

my mother told me about;

I hope it doesn't last long.

The most beautiful woman in

the world can only give

what she is.

Before marriage date long with

third eye open, antennas raised;

Compatibility tested in myriad

seasons to see if love wears

like a favorite robe.

To know your mother,

read her diary after she's gone.

If I practice self-denial,

how can I love my neighbor as

myself?

Love should not be blind

but four-eyed.

Time has changed my life songs;

every year a different melody,

slower and more thought out.

There is a tree called religion.

Its bough is covered in soot;

Its trunk splattered with blood;

On its leaves hang the

crucifixes of humanity.

Taste its shiny, bitter fruit.

Dare to look upon this tree

called Religion.

He said, "Good morning,"

and meant it.

There is splendor

in small things.

I've moved to a warmer

climate and must let go of my

woolen garments.

Consider the woman

who finds peace

upon the death

of her mother.

They say old Sadie went crazy

and started wearing short red

dresses; making up

her own rules and telling

the priest to confess his sins.

What if we could hold

the innocence of the baby

as we age?

I'd like to see you again

and take up the story

I tried to tell you

before we grew apart.

She looked behind the years

at the grown son; the little boy

chasing butterflies in the garden

before life's crooked roads,

detours and canyons;

before the bright eyes dimmed.

This is the heartbreak of

motherhood.

With laughter dancing at her

feet and freedom tied around

her waist, she strolls in peace;

unmarried and childless.

Grandparents look at the

grandchildren and rush

to become the parents

they should have been.

I took a seat with happiness;

Sorrow joined me and

whispered, "Don't get too

comfortable."

Let me not fall in love

but rise in love;

blinders removed and

reason intact; seeing clearly.

Things work out

so I won't make friends with

worry, that old trickster.

Even if death is the result,

things work out.

The child who is shown

tenderness becomes strong.

If he is shown compassion,

his heart can know empathy.

Why are we bound to earth,

if not to be wise stewards

of her life giving offerings?

A pauper spent his life

rebuking the rich,

and the mathematics of his mind

kept him poor.

The highest giver

expects nothing in return.

Create what you don't want

by dwelling on it.

The idea is the seed

expectancy, the fertilizer.

Divorce knocks but can't enter

the hearts of two people

flowing together and

growing in compatibility.

How can I say I love you

if I must turn you into

a carbon copy of myself?

To dream is to possess

Shangrila.

The answer to a prayer

will match the content

of the heart.

I have lived long enough to know why I didn't know the things I didn't know when I was young.

Aging is the mandatory

side effect of living.

Accept it as graciously as

your courage will let you.

The flower grows in the desert.

The sapling breaks

through rock.

I rejoice in my

power to overcome.

I love money

but it can't bring me peace.

Kudos to those

who do good

and never mention

their religion.

It's no small thing

for a human to die happy.

To know unconditional love;

consider the sunrise and the gift

of every new day.

Laughter that makes you cry;

ties your stomach in knots

while you gasp for breath

is good medicine.

One day her eyes opened

and she saw herself as others

saw her. The pain was too

great, so she put back on the

blinders and went again

to sleep.

If time takes my voice

and I can no longer sing,

I'll sit with closed eyes

and hear the melodies

that used to be mine.

*The past has slipped through my
fingers and my arms are too
short to hold the future.
So I hold close the present,
the only time I can call mine.*

I feel you thinking of me

when we're apart. It's

puzzling how when we meet,

you act as if I've never

crossed your mind.

A book

is the poor man's

vacation.

The wise mother knows her child. She does not force an artist to become a doctor; a teacher to become a CEO. She guides with ego intact.

Be grateful for the scars;

for they remind you

that the wounds weren't fatal.

The mind is a slave master

unless you rise up

and demand your freedom.

Great teachers are not in the

business of teaching;

but in the business of

helping students become their

own teachers and agents of

self-discovery.

Some days I just lie back and

daydream; no job, no children to

raise; no obligations I can't

shun; grateful to be in this

cycle of life called

old age.

I dare not rely on the history of

a country; written by experts

viewing the past through a

biased and distorted

sense of reality.

The dilemma of the world

is revealed in the

ruins of empires.

Forgiveness

can be an act of

self-preservation.

When I come to die,

let my love of all be intact;

money matters settled;

forgiveness well done.

I miss the old woman

who took me for walks

in woods that talked.

I squeezed her wizen hand

and she patted a blessing

on my head. She told me of the

promise in the stars and lulled

me with the cosmic song.

Humans create Gods in their

own image so they can justify

brutality and subjugate

those with different beliefs

and faces unlike their own.

We should be less afraid the

longer we live;

for we have wrestled with

life's monsters and prevailed.

She left home to find out what

the world could teach.

The leaving opened her too big;

and when she returned,

home would not fit.

Love takes all the

slavery out of you.

A hospice center

is full of forgiveness.

From moment to moment

we can only give

who we are.

A meal with a friend

does the body good.

Honest introspection

creates mastery

over one's life.

Unsung heroes

make the world go round.

The god of time

is now.